Would You Believe It About Animals

by John and Jackie Runeckles,
Rose Girling and Rick Sanders

Illustrated by Bill Tidy

FUTURA PUBLICATIONS LIMITED

A Futura Book

A Futura Book

First published by Futura Publications Limited in 1977

ISBN 0 8600 7581 8

Printed in Great Britain by
The Anchor Press Ltd
Tiptree, Essex

Futura Publications Limited
110 Warner Road, Camberwell
London SE5

At the height of his career, chimpanzee J. Fred Muggs had a US television audience of eight million and a weekly salary of £357.

Lewis Foley, who sells lion cubs at £250 apiece or £350 a pair, claims they are cheaper to feed than dogs. 'You just buy old battery hens or get a load of cow and sheep heads from the local abattoir and thrown them in,' he says.

The American Humane Association annually awards Oscar-style 'Patsies' for outstanding dramatic performances by animals.

The first dog member of the Co-op was Sultan Fisher, dividend number 27456, a 16-stone mastiff from York.

Lord Rothschild, the great naturalist, had a team of zebras to pull his carriage.

Julius Caesar's excuse for invading Britain was to take the pearls from our freshwater mussels.

Over-excited baboons have been seen trying to mate with foxes, cats, dogs and snakes.

Miss Farff, an English animal lover, trained her seal to recognize the meaning of 35 words; her two otters understood 18 and 16 words respectively, a rat learned six, and two squirrels knew five words each.

On the ruby-throated hummingbird's migratory flight from the eastern USA to South America it beats its wings 50 times a second for more than 2,000 miles.

A weasel family can support itself with a hunting territory of ten acres but a stoat household needs a hundred.

When Dr K. P. Schmidt was bitten by one of his laboratory snakes, a supposedly harmless boomslang, he meticulously recorded his bleeding gums, aching stomach and vomiting. It was left to others to record his death the next day.

When an experimental party of string and wind instrumentalists toured the cages at London Zoo, by far their most appreciative listeners were the crocodiles and alligators. They rushed out of their ponds when the band struck up a slow, mournful air and remained motionless on the bank with heads raised until the last strains had died away. The same tune infuriated the rhino and bored the cheetah – which did, however, respond favourably to some hot jazz.

The last duck-billed platypus sent to Britain was a war-time gift to Churchill. It died at Liverpool docks.
There are no hedgehogs in the Americas.

Gibbons as well as birds sing in dawn chorus. Their song always begins in the key of E, rising up the scale one octave in half an hour and descending again.

An otter's footprint is called a seal.
Sharks grow a non-stop supply of new teeth. A ten-year-old tiger shark will have used and shed 24,000.

The Warden at the Royal Society for the Protection of Birds' headquarters in Bedfordshire is John Partridge. Among his assistants are Barbara Buzzard, Celia and Helen Peacock, Dorothy Rook and A. Bird.

Such was the Oriental love of insect music that Chinese and Japanese took their favourite grasshoppers to work in cages.

Experiments by Dr Virginia Maiorana of the University of California prove that a salamander with its tail cut off is less likely to breed.

Some of the Federal US grants for 1974 were: 6,000 dollars to investigate the bisexual behaviour of Polish frogs; 20,324 dollars to study the mating calls of Central American toads, and 20,000 dollars to study blood groups of Polish Zlotnika pigs.

Lt.-Col. 'Elephant Bill' Williams reports that domestic elephants in Burma clogged the bells around their neck with mud when they wished to sneak off into the night to steal bananas.

Contraceptive birdseed cut the Paris pigeon population from 750,000 to 20,000 in four years.

Are elephants really afraid of mice? Frankfurt Zoo's attempt to find out ended when one of five mildly curious jumbos accidentally trod on the experimental rodent. A black rabbit, however, was utterly unimpressed by the trumpeting elephants and threw them into panic.

New Zealand's only native mammals are bats.

It was believed in the Middle Ages that a squirrel could leap from tree to tree all the way across Britain, from North to Irish seas, without once touching the ground.

Though elephants and hippopotamuses love water, neither can swim. Elephants use their trunks as snorkels while hippos run submerged along the bed, occasionally coming up for air.

There is a Malayan tick which works up its appetite by drilling through tortoises' shells before feeding on their blood.

Salmon fishery workers know when a seal has eaten a fish by a tell-tale ring of oil rising to the surface.

A survey by the Weser-Ems Chamber of Commerce in West Germany conclusively proves that hens make better peckers than cocks. Hens pecking at grains had a first-strike accurracy of between 48 and 82 per cent; cocks managed only 14 to 52 per cent.

In the US state of Maryland you can be fined for mal-treating an oyster.

An adult manatee chomps throught 60–100lb. of seaweed a day.

Common in the south-western USA, sleepy grass makes cows very drowsy, sometimes to the point of standing motionless for up to an hour. Once they have recovered their senses they will not touch it again, though sheep and horses happily get stoned on the grass repeatedly.

About half of Britain's 18 million households have pets – there are approximately 5.2 million dogs, 3.7 million cats, 3.3 million budgies, 10.5 million tropical fish, 5 million goldfish and a million rabbits.

Frank Hall, of Northumberland, was thwarted in his plan to stage a pie-eating competition with a pig. Too cruel to the pig, said the RSPCA.

A proposal that rent collectors in South Wales should be armed with electric prodders was dropped after pressure from the Canine Defence League.

Giraffe saliva has the consistency of soft rubber.

The famous Michelin guide now has a companion volume, the *Guide Mi Chien*. It supplies detailed information for travellers with dogs.

Despite being struck on the head nine times with a meat cleaver, police dog Otto held on to a burglar until he was arrested. Otto then 'died' from loss of blood, but made a full recovery after heart massage and mouth-to-mouth resuscitation.

Plastic pipes in the bar of a British Legion club had to be covered with metal tubing after mice had nibbled through and liberated 56 gallons of beer.

The royal Pekingese puppies of Imperial China were suckled by human wet-nurses, whose own 'superfluous' female children were drowned.

A letter to a magazine asked for confirmation that, according to Christian principle, the writer was correct in not allowing his budgerigar to use its swing on Sundays.

Dung beetles can trundle balls of goat and cattle dung several times their own size. In honour of this talent, the ancient Egyptians sanctified them as symbols of the force that turns the world.

———————•———————

Salmon was once so plentiful that British apprentices complained at being given it twice a week.

———————•———————

An insect-eating falcon can spot a dragonfly at a distance of half a mile.

———————•———————

Paris has 80 flushing lavatories for dogs.

———————•———————

A chimpanzee in a siver-lamé unisex jump-suit clocked 9 hours 52 minutes in the 1969 Daily Mail Transatlantic Air Race.

———————•———————

Albert the Great trained live dogs to act as candlesticks, holding the wax in their teeth while he ate his dinner.

500 dollars for proof of a single shark attack on a living man.

Attempts to mate chimpanzees and orang-utans at Chessington Zoo failed because the animals had never seen older animals from which to learn the arts of love. The zoo appealed to the BBC and film libraries for instructional film of apes making love in the wild.

In 1960, 169 Germans were killed by horses, cattle and pigs.

Thousands of robins descend on San Francisco every January and gorge themselves on pyracantha berries. Intoxicated, they then stagger about the roads, crashing into traffic.

A clumsy shark collided with the Australian guided missile destroyer Hobart and managed to break its SONAR equipment.

Kiwis are the only birds with a sense of smell.

Acupuncture has been successfully used in the USA to cure a breeding boar of arthritis and a dying horse of chronic emphysema. The horse recovered so quickly that on the third day of treatment it bolted in fear of the vet's needles.

A lamp-post in Gourock, Scotland, took a terrible revenge on its unwanted callers. It electrocuted three dogs, provoked another to bite its lady owner and sent an investigating policeman away with a painful shock.

A bashful heifer named Gesine provoked an international incident when her West German owners introduced her to a bull at Luchow. She took one look at her proposed lover, plunged into the River Elbe and swam 150 yards to the waiting East Germans on the other side, who declined to hand her back.

The kuri, a breed of humpless cattle who live on the shores of Lake Chad, have inflated spongy horns to keep their heads above water when swimming in search of feeding grounds.

A worried horse-owner appealed for help to horse tele-pathist Henry Blake after his mare had developed the habit of squealing, shaking her hind legs and urinating every time he entered her stall. Simple, said Mr Blake; she wants you to make love to her.

There is a steady demand for badger heads to make dress sporrans for the officers of the Argyll and Sutherland Highlanders.

After a farm truck containing 35 pigs crashed into a brewery wagon at Cologne, West Germany, it took police an hour to round up the drunken pigs.

Raccoons wash their food before eating it – usually in water dirtier than the food itself.

An American woman sent invitations to her husband's 30,000-dollar funeral not only to friends but also their pets. Her own two cats wore black ribbons while her poodle sported black collar, black leather bootees and black velvet fur-lined coat and cap. Their pitiful grief-stricken wailings at the ceremony were encouraged by starving them for the preceding 24 hours.

———————

Pyemotis mites are born sexually mature. Young males remain attached near their mother's genital duct, awaiting the birth of a sister. As soon as she arrives, her brothers pounce on her and copulate.

———————

Amos, a Staffordshire bull terrier from Tadworth, Surrey, eats only kosher food.

———————

It was believed by at least one medieval writer that badgers could run best on hilly ground because their legs were shorter on one side than the other.

———————

There are 25 different species of earthworm in Britain.

———————

Snakes are deaf. Charmers use rhythmic body movements to mesmerize their cobras. The music is just for show.

Mr Eric Titly's labrador leapt into the River Severn near Shrewsbury and emerged with a nine-pound salmon in its mouth. A passing inspector from the Severn River Authority seized the fish, saying it should be thrown back. When Mr Titly pointed out that it was dead, the inspector said in that case it should be buried. The salmon was finally placed in deep-freeze and a receipt issued to Mr Titly's dog. 'If one dog is allowed to go fishing, pretty soon half the dogs in the country will be up to it,' said an Authority spokesman.

Colonel Wilkins of Camberley was in the habit of feeding his grass snake on dead mice. When he gave it a live one as a treat one day, the meat proved too strong. It fought its way out of the snake's jaws and walked off.

Crickets' ears are on their front legs.

Four guests decided to travel by elephant to a wedding in Uttar Pradesh, India. On the way, they shared their drinks with their transport, who blundered into a power line, killing all five outright.

Chelmsford housewife Mrs Beryl Cheame dialled 999 when she heard high-pitched screams from the house next door. Police rushed to the scene to find Wilfrid, a hedgehog, with his head wedged in a can of baked beans.

A tunnelling mole can shift ten pounds of soil – about 50 times its own weight – in 20 minutes. To compete in the same league, a 12-stone miner would have to shovel four tons in the same time.

A male silkworm moth can smell a female seven miles away.

Bitch otters swimming in line with their young are blamed for many of the reported sightings of humped sea monsters.

World War Two acoustic mines on the Pacific coast were frequently detonated by fish calling to each other.

A mysterious influenza-like disease threatened a series of concerts by singer Roy Harper. Rushed to the local hospital's isolation unit, his ailment was diagnosed as toxopasmosis, a rare disease found only in sheep. Harper, who runs a farm between engagements, had recently given the kiss of life to an ailing ewe.

Saying they would rather be homeless than dogless, a couple offered their £4,000 house as a reward for their missing labrador bitch.

It is a rough rule among animals that the colder the climate, the shorter the legs.

Newborn kangaroos are about three-quarters of an inch long.

A pillar in London Zoo's old giraffe house was dented by an animal attempting to butt its keeper.

Before 1914, large quantities of common snails were eaten by Bristol glass-blowers as a means of improving their lung-power. Around the same time, tuberculosis sufferers were also encourged to consume a medicinal blend of snail-slime and sugar.

Drunken elephants have been terrorizing a Tanzanian game reserve after monster binges on fermented fruit. The tipsy tuskers apparently like nothing better than a wild trumpet chorus followed by a homeward orgy of uprooting trees and chasing smaller animals.

Ross, a labrador expelled from the school for guide dogs for his belligerence, joined the Royal Marines where he was ceremonially awarded a green collar – canine equivalent of the human commando's green beret.

Sitatunga antelopes can sleep underwater.

Modern chamois leather is more sham than shammy – it comes from domestic goats and sheep.

Each of the five dolphins who played Flipper in the TV series died of loneliness and boredom.

The octopuses of Monterey Bay, California, have recently taken to making their homes in discarded beer cans.

With a population of some three billion, the domestic fowl is the most abundant bird on earth.

An exhibition at the Turnpike Gallery, Leigh, featured 26 paintings specially produced for dogs. Priced between £1,500 and £3,000 and with such subject matter as sausages and bones, they were hung 18 inches from the floor. Dogs, normally banned from the gallery, were on this occasion admitted as long as they were accompanied by a human.

Huddersfield detectives had to interpret hoofprints to piece together the mysterious death of 75-year-old Mrs Alice Mellor, a farmer's wife. After approaching a new-born calf in a thunderstorm, the panicking mother had knocked her over and knelt on her chest.

A New York pet dealer says he sells remarkably few cats to negroes and orthodox Jews.

Impalas, a nervous species, make love on the gallop at up to 30mph.

It used to be considered a sign of good health to be infested with lice. They flee from a feverish body like rats from a sinking ship.

A zoologist at Leeds University has calculated, from the dimensions of fossilized footprints, that dinosaurs' cruising speeds varied between 2.2 and 11.7 miles per hour.

The expression 'rat-race' probably derives from the rat matches which were common in 19th-century London. Trained dogs were put into an arena containing up to 50 rats while onlookers placed bets on the numbers of rats that would be killed, within a time-limit. The most famous ratter, a dog called Billy, is reputed to have killed 500 rats in five-and-a-half minutes.

Female spiders often eat the male after mating, but one species has evolved so that the male ties down his mate first in the hope of making his escape while she is still untangling herself.

Shrews are easily frightened to death. Given a severe shock, their pulse rate is liable to soar to 1,000 beats a minute and more.

Members of the Tail Waggers' Club are promoted to the rank of centurion when their owners have recruited a hundred new members to the club. Lesser ranks include those of tailwagger corporal, sergeant and sergeant-major.

Mother koalas wean their young on a special eucalyptus soup served direct from the anus.

Certain types of ant steal eggs from other species and rear the young as slaves.

Rats stole 25 dollars in notes from a bank in Worcester, Massachusetts, and used it to literally line their nest.

Mr Heywood, rat-catcher, of Corby in Northants, has a special whistle to lure his rodent victims over contact poison.

A two-and-a-half foot koala bear may contain an eight-foot appendix.

Frozen beef and mutton first arrived in England from Australia in 1879. Frozen New Zealand lamb made its debut a year later.

Sloths camouflage themselves with festoons of green slime that grows in their coats.

A Brighton clairvoyant is noted for casting animal horo-scopes and reading paws.

Manta rays shake off troublesome parasites by taking great leaps 15 feet high out of the water.

Betty Andrews of Norfolk, Virginia, was distressed to find that the pet rabbit she donated to the local zoo had not been put on display to the public but fed to a python.

A shivering cow, rescued by the fire brigade after four hours trapped in a pond at Warmington, Northants, was given a bottle of brandy to cheer it up.

Sand lizards lift alternate feet into the air to stop them being burned by hot sand.

Earthworms excrete between eight and fifteen tons of new soil per acre per year.

Among the products you can buy for your dog or cat in the USA are trench coats, vinyl mackintoshes, sweaters, mink stoles and gold and silver boots. For beauty care there are perfumes, deodorants, hair tints, cream rinses, toothpaste, bad breath tablets and wigs.

Detectives of the world take note! Eels have a keener sense of smell than any dog.

The right whale was so named by whalers because of its slow speed and convenient habit of floating to the surface when dead.

Toby, canine soloist at a service for animals at St Paul's, Covent Garden, had his poor performance excused by his mistress – she said he was suffering from a sore throat.

A party of schoolchildren and five hamsters travelling from Southampton to Waterloo were charged an extra 50 pence per hamster by British Rail.

Progressive Argentinian ranchers have found that cattle fitted with chromium-cobalt false teeth are 25 per cent more fertile than those with their own teeth.

A great success in Drury Lane in 1840 was Molly the Whistling Oyster.

The aorta of a blue whale is large enough for a child to crawl through. The whale's body contains 15,750 pints of blood – enough to fill the veins of 2,000 humans.

Mice and rats eat more food each year than do half the population of the United States.

The contents of an osprey's nest in author John Steinbeck's garden included shirts, a towel, an arrow and a garden rake.

The outstanding champion King Charles spaniel of Victorian times was sired by a dog named after Charlie Peace, the notorious murderer.

An Australian forester was attacked by a koala who mistook the noise of his chain-saw for the territorial cry of another koala.

The Natural History Museum's unique collection of pickled snakes was evacuated to caves in Surrey during World War II.

A San Franciscan vet was sued for 226,100 dollars after the death of one of his poodle patients.

Mallards have been seen to catch sparrows in their bills, drown them, pluck them and then eat them.

Mr P. Davis' gelding Rodger alarmed so many passing motorists by sleeping on his back with his legs in the air and mouth open that Mr Davis put a large sign in his meadow saying THIS HORSE IS NOT DEAD.

Divorce was granted to a Californian woman after her husband had tried to make her put her foot into an orange box containing rattlesnakes.

A quarter of all mammalian species are able to fly. Man is one; the others are all bats.

Researchers in Wyoming, trying to find a way of making sheep unappetizing to coyotes, planned to use a £100,000 grant to spray flocks with synthetic Tabasco sauce.

A spider can spin 150 yards of silk in an hour and a quarter.

Whalers stranded by ice in Mackenzie Bay attempted to pass the time with a game of baseball but had to retire when a snowblind polar bear wandered into the game.

Favourite haunt of the black widow, the world's most poisonous spider, is beneath the seats of outside toilets.

The male Australian marsupial mole *Antichinus stuarti* has a mating season which lasts for only four days in June. After this, all males of the species die, thanks to a massive increase of certain hormones brought on by copulation. The litters produced by this ultimate sacrifice for love contain males for the next year's breeding.

Bacon beetle maggots perform a useful service to museum keepers preparing the skeletons of small animals – they are highly adept at eating away all traces of flesh from fragile skeletons without disturbing a single tiny bone.

Hippos confound their enemies by opening their mouths and blasting out foul gases from their stomachs.

The nobody crab is so named because it has no body.

A Cologne woman who promised 'an ecstatic night of lovemaking' to the man who found her lost Yorkshire terrier was surprised when her errant pet turned up on the doorstep in the company of the entire local fire brigade. The lady managed to dampen their expectant flames with a round of drinks.

A fieldmouse can jump to the ground from heights of up to 20ft without injuring itself.

When the Archbishop of Canterbury shot a gamekeeper while out hunting in 1613, King James I consoled him with the thought that it could happen to anyone. Indeed, he said, the Queen had recently committed a precisely similar offence by killing the king's favourite dog.

A cat that left a New York skyscraper by the direct route – through an 18th floor window – broke two legs and injured a lung, but survived.

Eskimo women never comb their hair on the day a polar bear is to be killed.

Movement in dogs' ears is controlled by a system of 17 different muscles. Humans have only nine ear-muscles. most of which are usually non-functioning.

On the evening that Sir Robert Grant, Governor of Bombay, died in 1838, a cat was seen to leave Government House by the front door and to walk Sir Robert's normal route. As the Hindus' sense of etiquette was every bit as strong as their belief in reincarnation, each cat that passed through the front door during the next 25 years was addressed as His Excellency and saluted.

An Indian railway worker in Honduras died two hours after being bitten by a *fer de lance* snake – despite the efforts of his wife, who hurried to bathe his wounds. But the widow's grief was short-lived. She died the next morning from venom that had entered her fingertips through a graze inflicted by a nutmeg grater.

A survey of kingfisher mortality revealed that seven had been killed by cats, two by passing trains and one individualist had drowned in a jar of tiddlers.

Female roe deer have white spots beneath their tails to help their young recognize them. All German bicycles have white rear mudguards. There is much bewilderment on German country roads.

Scavenging kites were protected birds in medieval London and often went into butchers' shops to help themselves to meat.

Cannabis can stunt growth! Dope-fed caterpillars take nine months to grow from egg to chrysalis. Their unstoned brethren do it in nine weeks.

The British public spontaneously donated five cwt. of sugar lumps and a ton of hay to the police horses which helped defend the US Embassy in London's Grosvenor Square against demonstrators in 1969.

Female giraffes are not passionate lovers. They often walk away in mid-copulation, leaving the unwary male to totter to the ground.

An American company was recently prosecuted for claiming that its brand of rattlesnake oil cured deafness.

A young brush-tailed porcupine in Sierra Leone became increasingly restless and distraught until one day it stole a lavatory brush and curled up beside it. It wanted its mother.

When rats were experimentally fed for six weeks on nothing but mushrooms, they put on weight.

In 1574 the water-mills on the River Severn were clogged to a standstill by a plague of cockchafer beetles that fell into the river.

In some species of birds the eyeballs are so large that they touch each other when moving about inside the birds' head.

During the American Civil War bat dung was mined as an ingredient of gunpowder.

The combined efforts of the RSPCA and the NSPCC convinced an East London father that two four-foot alligators were not suitable pets for his five-year-old daughter and he agreed to find them a new home. The following week worried residents read in their local paper that two alligators had been found in a nearby pond.

Mrs Gladys Emms of Mundford, Norfolk, suffered a mild shock when a thirsty mole crawled up the plughole of her kitchen sink.

If a tit is to survive the winter it must find a piece of food every two-and-a-half seconds for more than 90 per cent of daylight hours.

Mindful of their responsibilities in surroundings of unblemished scenic beauty, Gentoo penguins leave only pink droppings.

The patron saint of cows is St Bridget. She also watches over fugitives, midwives, newborn babies and Irish nuns.

Cambridge police received a number of alarm calls after a rat had been seen in the centre of Burleigh Street with its head stuck in a yoghourt pot.

An American Indian hired his snapping turtle to the local police whenever they needed to locate a drowned corpse.

Hen canaries can sing only if they are sterile.

The flatworm has a more than averagely useful penis. The organ emerges from the mouth and is armed with spikes and poison glands to catch prey.

The British Museum was startled when a supposedly dead African snail twitched its feelers and began to crawl after four years attached to an exhibition card.

"BY GEORGE! LET'S GET OVER TO THE MUMMIES JUST IN CASE!"

Henry VIII kept a polar bear which was allowed out on a chain to catch its own salmon from the River Thames.

Caesar's *Gallic Wars* includes a description of a method for catching elks in which trees are half sawn through, so that when the animals lean against them to sleep the trees fall over, taking the elks with them.

Brazilian hiccup fish are audible at a distance of one mile.

Muhamed, a German horse of the late 19th century, could apparently work out cube roots with a sack over his head. He tapped out tens with one hoof and units with the other.

It took a gang of workmen five hours with pneumatic drills, excavator and roadbreaker to shift 20 tons of rubble from a 15 foot hole and rescue a Jack Russell terrier from a drain under the A629 near Huddersfield.

A single wren has been seen to feed her young 1,217 times between sunrise and sunset.

Peter, the Home Office cat, was paid £6.50 a year to liquidate rodent enemies of the State. When he died in 1964, he was buried in an oak coffin at the PDSA cemetery in Ilford, Essex, with a marble memorial and an officially-mourning goat in ceremonial robes.

Looting polar bears are one of the hazards of Arctic exploration – they have been known to steal and eat coffee, rope, tobacco, canvas and rubber sheeting. On one occasion when a bear was followed, he was seen some miles from the scene of the crime excreting a complete but by then unwound reel of film.

The last time a blunderbuss was fired in anger in Britain was to dissuade an escaped lioness from attacking a passing stagecoach's horses.

At least twice as many male hedgehogs are born as females.

An escaped chimpanzee from Regent's Park made his way to Albany Street, hopped on a No. 3 bus and found a vacant seat. When the passenger beside him screamed, he bit her.

The birth of grey seal pups is an explosive business, accompanied by a noise like the popping of champagne corks. They land well clear of their mothers.

Solomon Islanders have evolved a novel way to catch dolphins; they bang stones together underwater, the noise of which drives the creatures ashore to bury their heads in the sand.

Mr Frank Mole was tending his roses when a fox sped across his garden into his living room. It was followed by a pack of hounds who tore it to pieces in front of the fireplace.

Being provided with only an incomplete set of intestines, an insect called the ant-lion is unable to defecate in the usual way and has developed a devilish alternative: it does all its digestive work in its saliva, which it then injects into its prey.

A woman was granted a divorce on the grounds of mental cruelty; her husband's boa constrictor shared their bed and mealtimes, when he fed it live mice.

Americans spend more on nourishing their dogs than they do on feeding their babies.

A popular Jacobite toast was to 'the little gentleman in black velvet' – the mole whose hole unhorsed and killed William III in 1702.

An occupational hazard of donkeyhood is to be allergic to buttercups.

The first recorded surgical operation at London Zoo was on a baboon with a decaying tooth in 1837.

South Shields Girls' Grammar School had to abandon their sports day because of dive-bombing herring gulls.

H.M. Inspector of Taxes required income tax at the standard rate to be paid on an annuity of £52 per annum left for the upkeep of Toby, a mongrel, by his former mistress.

Staff at the Maudsley Hospital in London's Camberwell fed stray cats with contraceptive pills hidden in food scraps.

Emperor penguins have been observed swimming at a depth of 870 feet.

It is a traditional Brazilian belief that putting a rattlesnake's rattle in a guitar not only improves the instrument's tone but also the owner's voice.

Mr Buthar Singh, an Indian travel agent, was using the placid surface of Lake Ranan as a shaving mirror when a playful freshwater turtle seized him by the nose and dragged him below the surface.

A helicopter made a mercy flight with 30 pounds of seed when Ebb and Flow, a pair of budgerigars living in the Shambles lighthouse off the Dorset coast, unexpectedly produced a family of four.

An elephant's trunk holds a gallon and a half of water.

Advice for young men in the colonies: F. B. Simson wrote in the 1880s that death is certain to follow a cobra bite 'unless perhaps if a bystander should have an axe in his hand and should chop off the limb a good way above the bite'.

Hedgehogs were popular Roman pets.

Goldfish fanciers have taken the trouble to breed a fish with no eyes.

Adélie penguins are liable to suffer from heat stress when the temperature rises above freezing point.

The carabid beetle of Alaska survives winter temperatures as low as $-40°C$ by making its own antifreeze.

To cut the accident rate on desert highways in the United Arab Emirates, free-ranging camels have been fitted with fluorescent jackets.

Dr J. Bond of the Agriculture Research Service of the US Dept. of Agriculture reported to the 134th meeting of the American Association for the Advancement of Science that Jersey cows' milk flow is interrupted for 30 minutes if paper bags are burst next to their ears.

Woodlice breathe through airholes in the last of their seven pairs of legs.

Punctuality is a fetish with many animals. One observer noted the same bat passing a particular spot at exactly five past nine for seven consecutive evenings. Another knew a porcupine which appeared at the same spot beside a lake at the same time every day for seven years.

From the reign of Edward II until 1972 all whales, dolphins, porpoises and sturgeons found on British beaches were legally the property of the reigning monarch.

The resourceful and talented Constable Judd of Ely deterred a herd of sheep from straying across a main road by impersonating a highly-trained sheepdog and barking them back to safety.

"HE DOES A VERY GOOD ALSATIAN AS WELL"

A rabbit was kept in an enclosure with an injured heron at a private zoo in Hertfordshire until the bird's plumage began to deteriorate. The rabbit had worn a patch trying to mount it.

Mrs Myrtl Grundt, a fur dealer's widow of Perth, Australia, left a million Australian dollars to two polar bears at the local zoo.

A Dorset innkeeper had a camel transported from Tibet to become a family pet.

'Terrapin' is a North American Indian word meaning 'eatable'.

A 23-foot basking shark cruising at two knots in his search for plankton will sift two million kilos of seawater per hour.

Locusts are too cold to fly first thing in the morning.

There are 4,200 known species of sponge.

An eight-week-old ferret can kill a fully-grown rabbit.

Beef cattle generally have a lower sex drive than dairy breeds.

Andean condors cannot hide their dishonourable intentions. Their heads and necks change from violet to bright yellow in the mating season.

Nearly 70 paintings by Betsy, a young female gorilla at Baltimore Zoo, were sold for up to 75 dollars each. The money was used to buy her a husband.

The most gluttonous mammal is the duck-billed platypus, which eats more food relative to its weight than any other.

0.000001 oz. of Colombian kokoi frog venom is enough to kill a man.

Two or three glowing glow worms put out enough light to read; in some parts of the world they have even been used as somewhat erratic bicycle lamps.

The oldest surviving breed of domestic dog is the saluki, which was used as a hunting dog in Mesopotamia before 300 BC.

Trains at Berne-Stoeckacker station in Switzerland had to be despatched by hand-signal after a neighbour's pet blackbird perfected its impression of a guard's whistle.

The title of 'Most Memorable Eyebrows of '76' was awarded to Lassie, the collie. Hers were hailed as 'more intelligent' than those of runners-up Elizabeth Taylor and US Vice-president Walter Mondale.

Chimpanzees Candy and Bonzo are nothing if not consistent ice-dancers – their colleague Jimmy always awards then 6.0 points. The only trouble, says trainer Werner Muller, is that their habit of licking the ice gives them colds in the stomach.

A Wiltshire girls' school protected the chastity of its pupils with patrolling guard dogs.

Two hundred bathers fled from the sea at Bournemouth in terror when teenage pranksters rowed past towing model shark fins.

When a 400-pound pig was lowered into a Brazilian river, piranhas stripped it to the bone in ten minutes.

Tranquillizers and aerosol deodorants are used on pig farms to minimize stress and conflict when newcomers are introduced into a pen.

Evolution is helping urban hedgehogs to survive. Instead of rolling into a ball, some advanced specimens have been seen running out of the way of oncoming cars.

"THAT'S EVOLUTION. ITS THE CARS THAT ROLL UP IN A BALL NOW!"

In the two weeks that Goldie the golden eagle was at large after escaping from London Zoo in 1965 he appeared on television over 100 times, caused huge traffic jams and made headlines in the world's papers. His two-week tour of London landmarks took him from Regent's Park to Lord's cricket ground, the London Planetarium and the Royal Academy of Music.

———————————

There is an old belief that any pig trying to swim would slit its own throat with its sharp front feet. It is incorrect.

———————————

Kookaburras tenderize lizards by nipping them steadily along the length of their body before swallowing them head first.

———————————

Once a snake has its teeth sunk into a meal, it can't let go. If two snakes start on the same meal from opposite ends, the larger keeps on swallowing and the smaller disappears.

———————————

There is no concrete evidence that cows ever go to sleep.

———————————

American naval divers have trained dolphins to protect anchorages from enemy frogmen.

———————————

Rats' incisor teeth keep growing at the rate of five inches a year.

———————————

Elephant teeth weigh up to nine pounds each.

Each of Frederick the Great's greyhounds had its own human servant, allowed to address his canine master or mistress only in terms of hushed respect.

Jim the Wonder Dog, a black and white setter from Sedalia, Missouri, predicted the winners of six Kentucky Derbys.

A column of Panamanian soldier ants which accidentally latched on to their own tail kept on marching round and round in a circle until they died of exhaustion.

Rhino urine is used as disinfectant in Southern Africa.

The combined opposition of bird-lovers and Yorkshire-men caused the council at Henley, Oxfordshire, to abandon its plan to round up the pigeons from the town hall roof and deport them to Yorkshire.

A blue whale's testicles can be up to 2' 6" long and weigh 100 pounds each. Its sperms, however, are no bigger than a man's.

The kangaroo rat of South-Western USA may go through life without tasting water.

New York police horses wear anti-slip rubber shoes.

An elephant called Anna May caused great problems for the make-up department when chosen to play the part of Jumbo in a film called *The Mighty Barnum*. The trouble was that Anna May was an Indian elephant whereas Jumbo had been an African, but it was overcome by fitting her with a large pair of false ears and some huge dummy tusks. Anna May's further claim to fame was her passion for onions, which she would crunch raw with tears rolling down her trunk.

The remora, a fish with a large oval sucker on top of its head, is used by fishermen in some parts of the world instead of a fish-hook. Thrown overboard attached to a line, it sticks its sucker to a large fish or turtle, which the angler then hauls in.

A thirsty camel can reduce the water-level of an oasis by 35 gallons in 10 minutes.

A particular type of segmented worm almost always swarms around Bermuda precisely 54 minutes after sunset on the third day after a full moon.

Octopuses have blue blood.

Baby Debrazza Gueron monkeys comfort themselves by sucking their thumbs.

Female whales' nipples are on their backs.

In Denmark, a cherry brandy company protects its cherry crop by amplifying a tape of a starling's distress call. It saves them £1,000 in fruit every season.

———————•—•———————

From the fall of the Roman Empire until the late Middle Ages, the official view of the church was that the ape was a diabolical beast. Since the devil could no nothing original, but merely mimic God, he became known as 'Simia Dei' – God's Ape.

———————•—•———————

Three common species of tapeworm are found in man: the beef, the pork, and the fish worm. The beef tapeworm has an average length of 24 feet and is known to have exceeded 80 feet. A Russian woman has been found harbouring six fish tapeworms with a total length of 97 yards.

———————•—•———————

Horned lizards can squirt blood from their eyes to a distance of 7 feet.

———————•—•———————

Danish pig breeders have produced a beast with two extra vertebrae to give more best back bacon.

———————•—•———————

An African park keeper saw a pride of five adult lions wait several hours while a lone zorilla – a harmless pole-cat – ate its fill from a zebra carcass. The lions dare not approach until the zorilla had left; and it was them that killed the zebra in the first place.

One of Napoleon's favourite sports was shooting the swans on Josephine's ornamental lake.

An old bull walrus is likely to have skin two-and-a-half inches thick.

———— • ————

Every golden hamster is a descendant of three members of a family of 13 dug up in Syria in 1930. The animal has never otherwise been found in the wild.

———— • ————

The herpetologist Klauber found that the severed heads of 13 rattlesnakes would bite sticks and draw their fangs for up to 40 minutes after decapitation. The headless bodies meanwhile did not attempt to rattle but squirmed a lot. One body righted itself from upside down after 7 hours 43 minutes; another's heart remained active after 59 hours.

———— • ————

The South American four-eyed fish can simultaneously see objects above and below the waterline with equal clarity.

———— • ————

No matter when badgers mate, the fertilized eggs will not begin to develop until December.

———— • ————

The chief hazard on the 17th green of a golf course at Redditch, Worcestershire, was a Burmese cat named Muang Putzi who selected the best balls – no split or dirty ones – and took them home.

———— • ————

Polar bears have been seen to cover their conspicuous black noses with a paw while out hunting.

A bee must visit about 100 flowers for a full load of nectar. 40,000 loads are needed for a pound of honey, which is about 50,000 bee miles flown and four million flowers visited.

———•———

Young gannets who stray from their parents' territory are stabbed to death by neighbours' beaks.

———•———

Bandicoot rats carry bubonic plague, scrub typhus, and rabies; and they can burrow through concrete.

———•———

The stomach contents of one contented grey shark — eight legs of mutton, half a ham, the hindquarters of a pig, the front half of a dog, 298 pounds of horse-meat, a ship's scraper and a piece of hessian.

———•———

The human flea can jump seven inches in the air.

———•———

The Natural History Museum in London has a piece of ship's timber into which a charging swordfish penetrated 22 inches.

———•———

At its trial for killing a child in 1572, an accused pig was dressed in human clothing. It was found guilty and sentenced to death.

taught a parrot to say 'Cézanne is a genius! Cézanne is a genius!'

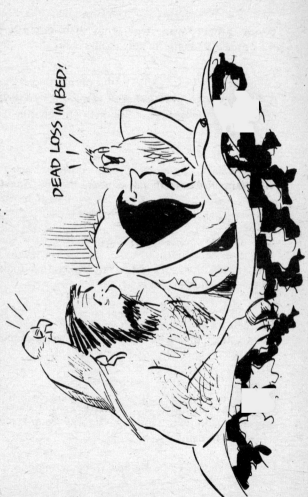

Eighteenth-century churchwardens commonly employed dog-catchers to keep their churches nuisance-free.

When a condemned prisoner in ancient Ethiopia was shown a painted owl it meant 'kindly kill yourself'.

When a squad of 36 rifle-toting Munich policemen finally tracked down an escaped wolf it was sitting quietly having its head stroked by a woman who had taken it for an alsatian dog.

Hummingbirds can fly backwards.

A South African railway signalman with a wooden leg taught a baboon to operate the signal levers for him. The animal also worked the rail trolley that took the pair of them to their signal box.

Earwigs lick their eggs to stop them going mouldy.

Salmon can high-jump more than six feet out of the water on their upstream spawning runs.

Giraffes can sleep lying-down for a maximum of five minutes.

It was Lyndon Johnson's daughter, Lynda Bird Johnson, who popularized a craze in the USA for wearing ear-rings consisting of two tiny bird-cages with a live bird inside. In France, meanwhile, fashion-conscious ladies were wearing ear-rings embellished by minute live South American snakes.

Goldfishes living in a group eat more water-fleas than solitary individuals.

In 1967 Muggins Carvey married Miss Petite Brabham at the Poodle Boutique, Palm Beach. The bride wore a satin gown trimmed with lace; her gay-dog groom sported a top hat and bow tie.

A single strand of spider-web spun around the world would weigh less than six ounces.

Barnacle geese are so-called because it was thought they grew out of barnacles.

The male camel's rutting display consists of expanding his tongue until it resembles a large balloon, hanging it from his mouth and loudly gurgling.

Police tracking down four cockatoos stolen from Cologne Zoo had one vital clue. All the birds spoke English with an Australian accent.

A five-course meal, crowned with strawberry-flavoured milk served from champagne bottles, was the high spot of an American poodle's coming of age (third birthday) party. All the guests were suitably dressed for the occasion: males in evening suits and patent leather boots, females in evening jackets with matching pants and expensive jewellery. Among the gifts were a musical box, a rubber postman and a cowboy outfit.

The first giraffe to reach Europe arrived at Marseilles in 1826. It was landed in the dead of night so as not to terrify the populace and finally reached Paris six months later.

——————— ·—· ———————

Ted Terry left Ketchum, Idaho, astride his bull Ohadi in July 1937 and arrived in New York's Times Square on August 11, 1940.

——————— ·—· ———————

Lion and tiger hybrids are known as tigons and ligers. Like mules, they are sterile.

——————— ·—· ———————

The animals at Karaganda Zoo in central Asia watched in dismay as their day's food disappeared into the stomachs of their keepers. Following the incident, the zoo director found himself replete but jobless.

——————— ·—· ———————

Natives in Indonesia believe that smoking through cigarette holders made from dugong tusks will protect them from bullets.

——————— ·—· ———————

Duck droppings are a favourite titbit of reindeer.

——————— ·—· ———————

Among many animals that have benefited from their owners' wills are a cockatoo and two leghorn fowl which shared £80,000 with various animal charities; a poodle which inherited £22,000; and a goat which received £115,000. The latter beneficiary in turn left the fortune to his late owner's nieces.

Homing pigeons have been known to find their way back to their lofts after absences of up to eight years.

Bananas laced with battery acid are among the weapons used by Ugandan elephant poachers.

Letchworth, Herts, has a colony of black squirrels.

The electric catfish can discharge up to 650 volts – more than 50 times better than the average car battery.

In the language of the Cewa, a Bantu-speaking people of eastern Zambia, the owl's hoot is 'Muphe! Muphe! Nimkukute!', which means 'Kill him! Kill him! That I may munch him!'

Mr Robin Chapman of East Dereham, Norfolk, caught a 12-pound cod with a packet of salt-and-vinegar crisps in its stomach.

Hares and humans have about 9,000 tastebuds on their tongues, while rabbits have 17,000 and pigs and goats 15,000. Rooks have 60.

Experimental research into the cause of ulcers involved the administering of electric shocks to two chained monkeys. One monkey alone was given a lever which he could pull to stop the current, and which he had to operate at least every 20 seconds for shifts of six hours on and six off. After 23 days he died of an ulcer. Further tests showed that the six-hour shifts were an essential ingredient of ulcers: bigger shocks and more intensive workloads produced no ulcers at all.

The world's oldest captive gorilla is aged 45.

Queen Elizabeth II succeeded to the British throne while watching elephants from the top of a Kenyan tree on February 6, 1952.

When angry, the Cuban boa turns red in the eye and bleeds at the mouth.

The word insect means 'in sections'.

Many rats and mice, like lizards, escape disaster by shedding their tails. The African dormouse, having a tail divided into eight-millimetre segments, can use this trick repeatedly.

A vital part of the porcupine's mating ritual is for the male to drench his partner with urine.

Mel Henderson, Professor of Art at a San Francisco university, set up 4,000 brightly-coloured artificial cows along Highway 80 between San Francisco and Reno. 'We wanted to do something to surprise and delight those who saw them,' he said.

The oldest recorded vulture lived to the age of 117.

over a single bank holiday weekend.

HOME MADE, EH. VERY NICE!

A tiger lizard under attack from a snake was seen to baffle its assailant by taking a hind leg in its mouth and forming a circle. The snake, used to swallowing lizards head first, did not know where to start.

After hearing strange noises during the final rinse, a Devon housewife investigated and found her pet cat in her automatic washing machine. The cat survived, but thereafter lost all interest in washing itself.

There are about five million laboratory experiments on animals in Britain each year, yet since the Cruelty to Animals Act was passed in 1876 there have been only three prosecutions against vivisectionists. Two were unsuccessful and the third resulted in a small fine.

To celebrate the wedding of Princess Sophia of Dresden to the Margrave of Brandenburg in 1662, George III of Saxony organized a gala hunt involving the slaughter of deer, dogs, bears and otters. Guests were all required to wear fancy dress; George himself chose to hunt as the goddess Diana.

Fortunately for predators, anchovies react to danger by massing thousands at a time into writhing spheres several feet across.

The aardvark, or earth-pig, defends itself against its favourite termite dinners by closing its nostrils. Ants, however, are more than it can cope with.

Foreplay to a sexually-aroused bedbug means piercing a hole in his mate's back with a spike on his penis. The sperm are ejaculated into the hole and swim through the female's bloodstream to her ovaries.

Grey squirrels have whiskers on their legs to help them feel their way when speeding through the branches.

Aristotle established to his satisfaction the fact that pointed eggs contained male chicks, and rounded eggs females.

Ants have five noses.

The bald eagle, emblematic bird of the United States, is bigger at the age of two years than when mature.

Lord and Lady Dowding owned a vegetarian poodle, that lived on nuts, cheese, raw carrots, egg yolks and biscuits. Wolf spiders have eight eyes.

Droopy doggy ears can now be permanently perked up – an American plastics company offers porous polythene inserts, sold slightly oversize in packs of two for vets to trim to size before implanting.

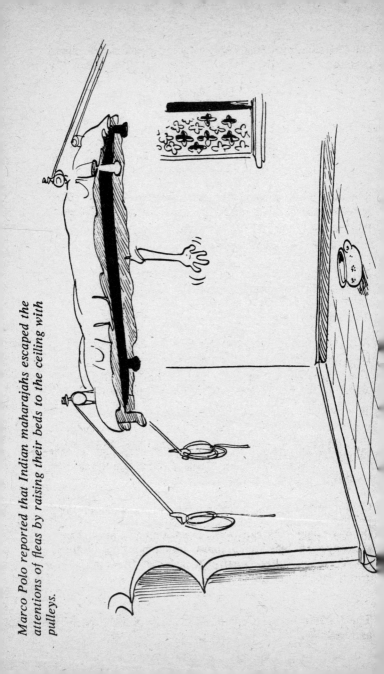

Marco Polo reported that Indian maharajahs escaped the attentions of fleas by raising their beds to the ceiling with pulleys.

On St Valentine's Day 1977, a swan in Hyde Park pined to death, a month after her mate had been killed by vandals.

In 1953, British poodles could get a special Coronation hairdo including flowers woven into the dog's coat.

Several US companies offer life insurance for cats. Each insured animal is identified by a nose-print in the company files.

Before eating a beaver, an American forest Indian will always remove the kneecaps and ceremonially burn them.

A mature female guinea worm is between three and four feet long. Males seldom exceed one inch.

The first ever dog show was at Newcastle in 1859. There were only two classes: pointers and setters. A judge in the pointer class won first prize for setters; and a setter judge won the pointer class.

Colour vision in most birds, monkeys and apes is comparable to that in humans. Horses, sheep, pigs and squirrels can distinguish a few colours; giraffes confuse green, orange and yellow; dogs and cats have some colour sense; but the golden hamster is totally colour blind.

The bulldog bat of Central and South America catches and eats fish.

Scorpions killed 20,352 people in Mexico between 1940 and 1949.

———— • ————

A German chain of maternity shops for dogs not only stocks canine maternity wear but provides luxurious facilities for delivery on the premises.

———— • ————

The average walking stride of an emu is three to four feet.

———— • ————

Among the problem guests catered for by a Munich holiday home for dogs were a bulldog who upended his morning milk if not laced with brandy and a spaniel who would only go to sleep when rocked to his favourite lullaby.

———— • ————

A captured python cut open in the royal palace in Bangkok revealed a royal Siamese cat, identified by a silver bell around its neck.

———— • ————

When Adélie penguins want to check the sea for danger, they line up on the ice and shuffle one of their number into the water. If the volunteer fails to return, they save their dip for later.

———— • ————

The upside-down catfish of the Nile is so called because it swims that way.

———— • ————

According to a Bell Telephone Co. advertisement, a depressed chimpanzee was considerably cheered when a telephone was installed in his cage.

chihuahua snuggled inside a woman's jumper, a shop-lifting accomplice ransacked the shelves.

Pope Gregory the Great (540–604) installed his favourite cat as a cardinal.

The bombardier beetle defends itself by firing a burst of caustic smoke from a vent at the rear of its body. The noxious mixture is given zest by hydrogen peroxide – one of the prime ingredients of rocket fuel.

A Devonshire woman stopped attending church because the Bishop ruled against her dog taking Holy Communion.

Fashion-conscious South American women feel undressed without their spider and beetle accessories. The be-jewelled spiders remain motionless through fear of the bright lights, but beetles – attached by lengths of gold chain – have the freedom of their wearers' shoulders.

England's east coast herring fishermen enjoy their heaviest catches during the full moons of October and November.

Coypus have been known to kill cats by luring them towards water and drowning them.

New-born New Forest foals frequently form strong filial attachments to moving cars – sometimes even to stationary objects like trees – and refuse to acknowledge their real mothers.

Two thousand caterpillars have been found in the stomach of a single emu.

World War One surgeons found that soldiers' wounds healed more rapidly if green-bottle maggots had been feeding on the putrefying flesh.

Among the popular names for the albatross are molly-mauk (from the Dutch 'stupid gull'), gooney bird, and bakadori (Japanese for 'fool bird').

A Preston doctor convicted of abandoning two lions and two baboons was fined and disqualified from keeping wild animals for one year. 'Life is no longer worth living,' he said after the trial.

Chimpanzees frequently greet each other with a hand-shake.

Barnacles growing on the hull can reduce the speed of a freshly-scoured battleship of 35,000 tons by a knot within the space of six months.

In just over a month, a pair of busy burying beetles interred two moles, four frogs, two birds, four grass-hoppers, some fish-gut and two pieces of calves' liver.

The giant dung beetle declines to eat or lay eggs in anything lesser than elephant droppings.

Among the 40,000 pets buried at the Hartsdale Caine Cemetery in Westchester, U.S.A. are monkeys, goldfish, parrots, cats, salamanders, a lion and a dog war hero buried wearing the uniform of a major.

THE UNKNOWN BUDGERIGAR

Scientist Dr Colin Blakemore, a recent Reith lecturer, took live kittens and rotated their eyes in their sockets by between 30 and 90 degrees in an experiment that proved beyond doubt that kittens with upside-down eyes bump into things.

Damage by rats costs Britain 25 million pounds a year.

Cigarette beetles in a Rentokil laboratory at East Grinstead were weaned off tobacco by a diet of dog biscuits.

The first thing Queen Victoria did after her coronation was to wash her favourite dog.

House mice survive inside cold-stores by growing thick woolly coats and building nests from pipe-lagging.

Some types of tapeworm can produce a million eggs a day for up to 20 years.

The nine-banded armadillo is in great demand as a laboratory guinea-pig, being the only creature apart from humans to suffer from leprosy.

Starfishes can exert a steady pull of three pounds – just enough to open an oyster.

HM The Queen, who owns all sturgeon caught in British waters, presented a live one to an aquarium in 1969 and a dead one the following year to an orphanage.

If the descendants of a single aphid all survived and multiplied, in a year their weight would equal that of 600,000,000 men.

Jellyfish are little more than organised water. Only 4% of their bulk is salts, and 1% organic matter; the rest is just wet.

Elegabalus, a teenage transvestite Roman emperor, was fond of a ritual, ostensibly for the sun-god, in which an ape, a lion and a snake were shut in a temple and ceremonially bombarded with human genitals.

Winston Churchill often took his cat to Cabinet meetings. Napoleon, on the other hand, would break out in a cold sweat at the sight of even the smallest kitten.

American TV advertisers have experimented with dog whistles at the beginning of commercials. They hoped that pets thus alerted would encourage their owners to buy the product.

Seals can suffer from seasickness if they ride in boats.

Dr Graves, an American poultry scientist, has found that chicks grow much faster in their first five weeks when exposed to high-voltage electrical fields.

... coaches ... from instructors' are attached them
selves to such unsuitable 'mothers' as large boxes and a
football.

As an aid to flight, birds' bones are hollow and fed with air from ducts connected to the lungs. It is thus possible that a bird could breathe through a broken bone.

Five hundred and sixty-one bats were counted departing from the roof of a house at Blandford, Dorset, on the evening of July 25, 1967.

A South African entry in the 1970 Cape Town to Rio yacht race was sunk by a whale.

Medieval doctors prescribed curled-up woodlice as pills for digestive complaints.

A snake that has just had a really good meal may not have another for as much as a year.

Homesick British émigrés introduced the starling to New Zealand in 1862, to Australia in the following year and to South Africa in 1898. The first starlings in America, where there are now probably 500 million, were liberated in New York Central Park in 1900 by a man who took the view that all the birds mentioned in Shakespeare should live wild in the USA.

Horses are immune to tear gas.

Some lizards keep cool in hot weather by urinating over themselves.

Between half and two-thirds of the five million annual experiments on animals in Britain are for such non-medical causes as testing cosmetics, chemicals and weapons.

It took three strong men to pull an ulcerated tusk from a hippo at London Zoo, tugging on a two-foot pair of forceps from the far side of a fence erected for their protection.

Penguins on land are very short-sighted, but can see well underwater.

St Evlavia died at the age of 12 after a lifetime dedicated to a daily ritual that involved catching all the fleas in her blankets, counting them, dividing them into males and females and then releasing them so that she could do it all again tomorrow.

At least 100 mammal species have become extinct during the last 2000 years, and the rate has now accelerated to around one a year. Among those currently most at risk are the Rusty Numbat, the Pig-footed Bandicoot and the Hairy-nosed Wombat.

Blue whales reach their massive weight of 130 tons on a diet of krill – a shrimp-like fish rarely more than 2in. long.

The humpback whale has been observed making love in three different positions.

There were so many caterpillars in the Tamar valley in 1955 that railway lines became slippery with their crushed bodies.

A poorly elephant may be suffering from diabetes, nettle-rash, pneumonia, peritonitis, flatulent colic (no doubt about this one), a cold or mumps.

The three winning jumps of the 1929 Californian frog-jumping derby totalled less than twelve inches.

There is a breed of spider that lies in wait for its prey disguised as a bird dropping.

When the first European sailing ships arrived with live-stock at the Marquesas islands, the natives, who had only pigs, took the new animals for strange varieties of porker. Thus they named the horse 'pig-running-fast-on-the-trail' and the goat 'pig-with-teeth-on-the-head'.

The council at Stamford, Lincolnshire, abandoned a plan to use guard dogs to deter vandals at a local cemetery. A council spokesman explained: 'We would be a laughing stock if we used dogs to guard dead people.'

So dear is the hunting falcon's love for its feeding place – the falconer's gloved hand – that it will furiously defend it against 'attack' from the man's face.

Britain has separate charities for the protection of animals in Italy, Spain, France, North Africa, Israel, Greece and Japan.

Giraffes give birth standing up, babies diving into the world feet first from a height of six feet.

The Masai of Kenya drink fresh cows' blood drawn from a vein in the living animals' necks.

Given total protection from predators and disease, one pair of rabbits would become 3½ million within three years.

A small worm exclusive to the hippopotamus lives under its eyelids and feeds on tears.

Swedish vets have produced a contraceptive injection for dogs.

It was believed in the Middle Ages that if you dropped horse hairs into liquid manure they would turn into poisonous snakes.

Some Pacific islanders kill sharks by boiling large melons and throwing them into the water with chopped fish. The sharks, attracted by blood, gulp down whatever they find, including the melons which, though cold outside, are still boiling within. The heat and expanding gas kill the shark and cause it to float conveniently to the surface.

Tiger, the cat at London's Ritz Hotel, is so grossly over-fed on aristocratic leftovers that every year it is sent on a fortnight's slimming course and health cure.

The flea circus of Signor Bertolotto, a resident attraction in Regent Street in the 1830s, included a 12 piece flea orchestra, a miniature mail coach with liveried flea coachman and flea horses, and, as a pièce de résistance, three fleas dressed as Wellington, Napoleon and Marshal Blucher.

"DATSA NAPOLEON GOING INTO EXILE!"

BERTOLOTTO'S FLEA CIRCUS

Judge Robert Lymbery had to be taken to hospital after over-ruling a magistrates' order for a 12-stone Great Dane to be destroyed. After hearing of his reprieve, the grateful beast bit him.

The most potent creature in the world is a rodent, *m-riones shawi*, which can copulate up to 224 times in two hours.

Gorillas never snore.

A recommended method of artificial respiration for cats is to take the animal by the tail and swing it back and forth to a regular count of four.

At the Texas Memorial Museum's Tarantula Tournament in 1970, there were prizes for the biggest, smallest and hairiest specimens submitted to the judges.

There are about 90 spines per square inch of hedgehog. Pebbles account for ten per cent of an adult crocodile's weight. This ballast makes the mature reptile a better swimmer than young ones with an incomplete collection of swallowed stones.

The BBC archives contain a recording of a starling saying 'Kiss me, cuddly, cuddly, cuddly, kiss me'.

To find out how many rabbits are using your back lawn as a public convenience, count the number of pellets deposited in 24 hours and divide by 360.

———— • ————

A dead shark was the key witness at an American privateer captain's trial in 1799. Chased though the Caribbean by a British man-of-war, he had tossed a roll of incriminating papers overboard – straight into the jaws of a lurking shark, which was duly hooked and gutted by his prosecutors.

———— • ————

Hatfield Rural District Council's Chief Rodent Officer put his dog on the payroll at £5 per annum after she had killed 15 rats inside an hour.

———— • ————

The gorilla is less of a man than many people imagine. Swiss zoo director Ernst Lang reveals that the beast's erect penis extends only to a measly 2in.

———— • ————

In the USA there are around 3000 cat and dog births per hour. The human rate is a paltry-by-comparison 450.

———— • ————

In Chinese cricket matches, the crickets were trained for combat on a diet of mosquitos bloated with blood – usually that of the owner, wishing to pass on his strength to his insects.

———— • ————

Cats and humans react in opposite ways to the drug morphine.

means food, 'cheny' means drink, and 'legk' means watch out!

The two heads of a freak garter snake in New York Zoo had to be kept apart by a cardboard collar to prevent their biting each other.

The weight of insects eaten by the world's spiders in a year is greater than the combined weight of every man, woman and child on earth.

While buildings all around were demolished, Louise the parrot lived on in lonely splendour – her owner's will stipulated that the house should stand until she died, and that she should be given two meals and a nip of brandy a day.

A dolphin swimming at 15 miles per hour uses as much energy as a human climbing Mont Blanc at five miles per hour.

Dr H. R. Bustard has calculated that a mother green turtle has to shift up to a ton of sand to lay her eggs.

Male rhinos eject their urine as puffs of highly pressurised spray. The cow's urine is also released with considerable force but in the form of a liquid jet.

Konrad Lorenz has trained flocks of geese to take off and land at his command. His air-traffic control system involves waving his arms, running and suddenly lying flat on the ground.

Big Ben was once prevented from striking nine o'clock by the weight of starlings perched on its hands.

The sight of a hosepipe is snake-like enough to make toads puff up in alarm to twice their normal size.

Housefly maggots outgrow their skins twice in their first week of life.

Wild chimpanzees spend less than 0.4 per cent of their time fighting.

In 1932 the Australian Army was called out to do battle with a huge migrating horde of emus. It killed a few hundred but the operation was not counted a success.

Boars have little interest in the opposite sex during hot weather, but if the animal is wetted, or if there is a chance of a wallow, libido immediately rises.

A country lane in Somerset was blocked with soil by badgers digging a new sett.

One African termite hill, crushed and mixed with water, yielded 450,000 tons of bricks and cement.

Ancient Indian armies fitted tridents to the horns of rhinos which they deployed as front-line battle tanks.

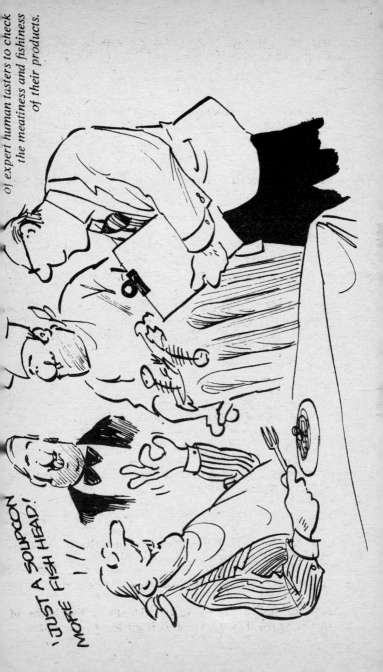

... of expert human tasters to check the meatiness and fishiness of their products.

'JUST A SOUPÇON MORE FISH HEAD!'

Geese have been seen over the Himalayas at 29,000 feet.

The spiky porcupine fish protects itself from predators by inflating itself with air or water and turning into an unswallowable prickly ball.

Wasps buzz at 110 wingbeats a second, houseflies at 190, mosquitos at 500 and midges at 1,000.

A grey squirrel broke into a Bournemouth flat to bury his nuts behind the chair cushions. The flat was on the 16th floor.

About 20,000 dogs a year are admitted to the Battersea Dogs' Home. About 60 per cent have to be destroyed.

When a naturalist attached small tracker radios to the backs of wild hedgehogs he was obliged by the 1949 Wireless and Telegraphy Act to licence each animal as a Testing and Development Station.

The lesser whistling tree duck builds its nest in tree-forks.

The indiscriminate appetite of the wolverine, largest of the weasel family, is reflected in its alternative name of glutton.

Dr. Boris Levinson, a New York professor of psychology, says that by the year 2000 humans will be served by animals with electrodes implanted in their brains. At the turn of a dial, he says, these living robots will open doors, close windows, make beds and even call out for help. Theft, robbery and murder will be committed by specially trained pets in the employ of racketeers.

The inhabitants of Bermuda use shark liver oil to forecast the weather. The oil, sealed in an airtight jar, turns cloudy before a storm, forming ridges and peaks before a really fierce blast. The best oil comes from puppy sharks; oil from nurse and hammerhead sharks is no good, though considered a very good cold cure.

It took a steamer 15 minutes to pass through a swarm of lemmings swimming off Trondheim, Norway, in 1868.

Mexican tree squirrels can survive a fall of 600 feet.

Unless owners specifically ask for the body, pets destroyed by vets are wrapped in plastic 'body-bags' and taken to the council tip.

Duck farmers have found that bantams' bottoms are better than electric incubators for hatching eggs.

The Kenyan Game Department has a $3\frac{1}{2}$ inch horn found growing from a rhino's backside.

Grey squirrels cause over a million dollars' worth of damage a year to electricity cables in the USA – they eat the plastic insulation.

During the height of the Blitz, a goat in Bermondsey set a world record for milk-production.

was a proud but unenthusiastic mother. After a quick glance at her new-born she invariably passed them disdainfully to the nearest keeper.

The Flying Steamer Duck of South America can run across the water at up to eight knots.

Government research revealed that cows and sheep adapt quickly to Concorde's sonic boom. After four bangs, cows showed little reaction. Sheep were a little jumpier, but a research worker said: 'My impression is that we have not worried them.'

One British dog in seven has worms.

A youth, fined £3 for hitting a policeman at three o'clock in the morning, claimed that he had been enraged by the noise of herring gulls in Sunderland town centre.

The sheep tick is a patient animal. After a meal it drops off its host and may wait four years for its next to happen by.

Charles Waterton, the first Englishman to build a bird sanctuary, used to catch pike in his private lake with a bow and curare-tipped arrows.

The word porpoise is derived from the French *porc poisson* – or 'pig-fish'.

Swan expert Oscar J. Merne, warden of the Slobs of Wexford reserve in Ireland, says swans can't break men's arms.

There is a hospital for sick fish at Toba, Japan.

———— ••• ————

The rare angwantibo, a relative of the bush baby found only in the Cameroons, can turn somersaults by walking through its hind legs.

———— ••• ————

Tanzania was once plagued with a swarm of locusts so big that it would have taken seven days and nights to kill them at the rate of a million per minute. The weight of numbers was enough to snap three-inch branches like matchsticks.

———— ••• ————

The only large mammal discovered this century was the okapi. Sir Harry Johnston was actually looking for a unicorn when he stumbled upon it by accident.

———— ••• ————

Modern turkeys are artificially inseminated, being unable to mate. When a turkey cock was experimentally put with battery females, they failed to recognize him and scattered in alarm.

———— ••• ————

The youngest of the three zeedonks in captivity is Mary, born in Christmas week 1975 at Colchester Zoo. Mary has the legs of a zebra and the body of a donkey.

———— ••• ————

In ancient Britain, the fine for insulting the King's Bard was six cows and eight pence.

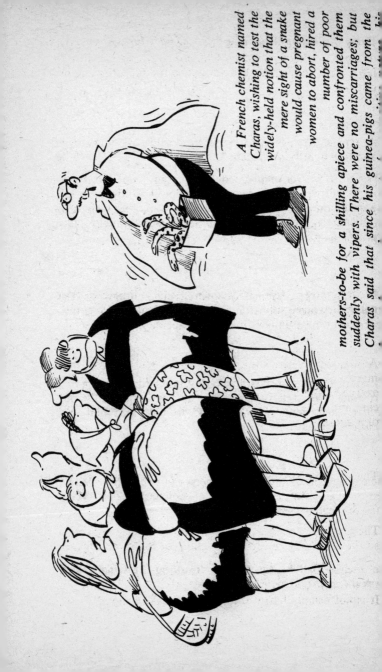

A French chemist named Charas, wishing to test the widely-held notion that the mere sight of a snake would cause pregnant women to abort, hired a number of poor mothers-to-be for a shilling apiece and confronted them suddenly with vipers. There were no miscarriages; but Charas said that since his guinea-pigs came from the

After observing that dogs are never worried by cold, damp or arthritis, modern Chinese doctors have formulated what they claim is a sure cure for the disease from dog bones.

A typical English field supports a spider population of about two million per acre.

A group of spectators at Coogee Aquarium, Sydney, were surprised to watch a tiger shark vomit up several pieces of partly-digested meat and a tattooed human arm.

It was only in the seventeenth century that European naturalists realized that queen bees were not kings.

A prisoner at Parkhurst kept a pet bumble bee in a matchbox. It always returned after being let out for exercise and had a particular fondness for its owner's ears and armpits, but died when accidentally shaken out of a blanket and trodden upon.

The average British chicken lays 230 eggs a year.

The Gelada baboon has its two nipples set close together so that the baby can feed from both at the same time.

It is not usually harmful to swallow snake venom.

Sally the performing hen convulsed her audiences by drinking beer, laying a dozen eggs in rapid succession and blowing up a green breathalyser. "A cheap gimmick", said Miss Irene Heaton, of the Captive Animals' Protection Society.

The giant squid drinks its victims alive; it grips them in its tentacles, punctures the skin with its beak, injects a saliva which dissolves the innards and sucks out the resultant sludge.

In California you can be fined 500 dollars for disturbing Monarch butterflies.

An ocelot which earned its keep as a ship's cat was lost overboard while trying to catch flying fish.

The Spanish nickname for sloths is 'nimble Peter'.

A Bonn schoolboy was questioned by police after performing a heart transplant on his pet mouse. He said it was a fairly simple two-hour job using aspirin as an anaesthetic, a model railway transformer as a heart booster and a breathing device of his own design.

Platypus milk seeps out through pores in the mother's abdomen.

Giraffe milk is seven times richer in protein than cows' milk.

protect their pets' eyes with Spratt's Motoring Goggles, specially designed for the sporting dog at 4/6d a pair.

A single cabbage white caterpillar has been found crawling with 150 parasitic wasp maggots and still alive.

Phantom pregnancy in goats is known as 'cloudburst' after the three gallons or so of pale fluid that issues forth when the 'mother's' time is up.

Hedgehog fleas do not hibernate with their host, but their breathing rate does slow down.

Some North American cuckoo flocks build a communal nest in which all the females lay their eggs.

Dr Leon Smith, thanks to his Behavioural Engineering Technique, has taught bears to play basketball – 'Food is now secondary to the thrill of making a score,' he says. He has also persuaded carp to smoke cigarettes through an underwater holder, to feed from a baby's bottle and to pick out the queen from a row of playing cards.

Scottish red deer eat frogs.

The hedgehog's brain is very similar to that of the kangaroo; young ones frequently spring into the air for no apparent reason.

The last wild wolf in France was killed in Isère in 1954.

When Namibian black-backed beetles mate, it takes three males to subdue one female.

Armadillo litters consist of identical twins of the same sex.

Using its mouth as a sucker and fins as levers, a South American catfish has been seen to climb a 20-foot wall in 30 minutes.

Locusts have been seen as far north as the Shetland and Orkney Isles.

Dick Whittington's cat was not an animal but a boat. He made his fortune with a fleet of cat-boats carrying coal from Newcastle to London.

Among the more colourful collective nouns for birds are: a murder of crows, a tok of capercaillie, a rush of pochard, a herd of wrens, a rafter of turkeys, a siege of herons, a deceit of lapwings and an unkindness of ravens. Also correct are: a business of ferrets or flies, a labour of moles, an erst of bees, a pod or gam of whales and a fluther, smack, smuth or stuck of jellyfish.

There is a South American millipede with 1,568 legs.

After 15 years, Otto Zuger of Muhlbach, Austria, finally succeeded in training a trout to leap into a beer mug.

When the water-ouzel has finished feeding on a river bed, it does not wait to surface before commencing to fly but starts beating its wings while still submerged.

The Romans had special containers in which they fattened dormice for the table.

A bee's eye has 6,300 lenses.

The grateful burghers of Freiburg, West Germany, erected a statue in honour of a duck. The bird had a reputation for making a fuss before an air-raid, and on November 17, 1944, it left its pen and waddled through the town anxiously squealing and quacking. Even though there had been no air-raid warning, people went to the shelters – just in time to escape the British bombers that arrived a few minutes later and devastated the town.

An eminent dental surgeon came to the rescue when a toucan at London Zoo had a piece of his beak bitten off by an uncooperative female. The dentist made an alloy frame covered with a plastic skin that was fixed to the stump of the beak with dental cement and coloured to match the original.

Elephants normally use only one of their tusks – some are right tusked, others left.

When young weasels are killed on the roads, parents drag the body off to cover.

Whales are the best animal high-jumpers. Some can clear 20 feet.

An unwillingly propositioned female echidna prods her spines at the male's genitals.

The philosopher Pliny maintained that eels were sexless and that they reproduced by rubbing themselves against rocks and chafing off pieces of skin that grew into elvers. Percy the tomcat was justifiably terrified of Goliath, a pet mouse, in Shaldon, Devon. Owner Mrs Irene Arnot had to give them separate saucers after the mouse bit a slice out of the cat's nose.

Indian rhino dungheaps, which receive a contribution from every animal that passes, may be 15 feet across and four feet high.

In 1486 Dame Juliana Berners wrote that the dogs of England were: 'a Greyhound, a Bastard, a Mongrel[1], a Mastiff, a Lemor, a Spangel, Raches, Teroures, Butchers' Hounds, Dunghyll dogges, Tryndeltaylles and Prycked curres, and smaller ladyes poppees that bare away the flees'.

Theo Brown discovered a good method of frightening sharks was to play Beatles' songs to them underwater.

A mole can bury itself in five seconds.

If you forget to pay the annual grave fee for two years at the Mexico City Dog Cemetery, your loved one will be dug up and thrown into a common pit, freeing valuable space for a better-loved one.

Cockatoos marauding in a field always leave one of their number up a tree as lookout. If he fails to remain alert, the others kill him.

The Chinese standard for Pekingese dogs advised owners: 'Let it be fed on sharks' fins, curlews' livers and breast of quail, and let it drink tea from the Spring buds of the bush that groweth in the Province of Han Kon, on the milk of antelopes that pasture in the imperial parks, or broth made from the nests of sea-swallows. Let it venerate its ancestors and deposit offerings in the Canine Cemetery of the Forbidden City on each new moon. Thus shall it preserve its integrity and self-respect.'

Pepe Zip, winner of the 2nd World International Snail Derby at Murillo de Rio Leza, near Barcelona, was subjected to a drug test after it was discovered that he had been soaked in Burgundy three minutes before the start of the race.

When forced to take to the water, nine-banded armadillos inflate their intestines as buoyancy tanks.

Giraffes have special valves in their necks to stop the blood rushing to their heads when they stoop to drink.

Among the unauthorized food gobbled by London Zoo animals one year were 14 coats, 12 handbags, 10 cameras, 8 gloves and 6 return tickets to Leicester.

Farmer Colin Newlove of Yorkshire has trained his bulls to jump hurdles, roll oil drums, sit, lie down, play dead and to be ridden through hoops of fire.

In 1916 a South Australian farmer put out poisoned mouse bait and next morning found on his verandah the corpses of 28,000 house mice.

There is a special supply of Evian's spa water reserved for dogs.

The potoroo, smallest of the kangaroo family, does not drink water and in hot weather perspires through its tail.

Though the average life-span of a herring gull is three years, one captive bird survived to the age of 44.

When placed against a wall, some hedgehogs always turn to the right, some to the left, while others can go either way.

If a bee succeeds in seducing his queen, his sexual organ snaps off inside her and he bleeds to death.

Within a day of being born, a fallow deer faun can out-run a man.

Gauche young bulls often exhaust themselves by repeatedly trying to mount cows from the side.

According to animal trainer Mary Chipperfield, the most trainable animals are, in order: chimpanzees, elephants, dogs, horses, lions, tigers, leopards and cheetahs. 'Gazelles and antelopes are pretty stupid,' says Miss Chipperfield, 'but bottom of the list I'd put the hippo. About the most you can teach a hippo is to stand still and let you feed it.' You can tell when a sow is in season by sitting astride her back. If she stands still and sharply pricks up her ears, she's ready.

Gecko lizards can't grip wet surfaces, so Australian naturalists hunt them with water-pistols.

Among the exhibits in the Athens Drug Squad's black museum is a duck stuffed with hashish.

When Tarzan left Florida after filming in 1934, three of his apes were left behind. To the disquiet of residents, their progeny now number more than a hundred and are so ferocious 'they could tear a man's arm off'.

A patient from a Sheffield mental hospital who walked 16 miles in carpet slippers before collapsing unconscious in a ditch was discovered by a lion out for a stroll with its owner.

The owner of Poopsie, a poodle, insisted that her pet be buried at the American Pet Memorial Cemetery in Florida wrapped in its favourite electric blanket.

A leading canine expert claims that dogs are emotionally damaged when their owners are over-affectionate in their presence.

The Russians in World War II combated the menace of German Panzer tanks by training dogs to run underneath them with explosive loads strapped to their backs.

The Mexican canary fish performs its musical air-bladder contractions in choirs several hundred strong.

Cheetahs can accelerate from 0–40 mph in two seconds.

Pigs' penises are about eighteen inches long, stallions' two foot six, bulls' three feet, elephants' five feet, and blue whales' seven or eight feet.

A blowfly's feet are five times as sensitive to sugar as its tongue.

The South American leaf-eared mouse, which eats cochineal beetles, has pink bones.

One tame hedgehog loved Jacob's cream crackers but refused other brands; another was seen in Kent lapping up battery acid.

Indian climbing perch make their way across the ground and up trees using spikes on their underside to give purchase while pushing forward with their fins and tail.

Among the deformities encouraged by breeding dogs to pedigree standard are dislocation of the lens in terriers, ingrowing eyelashes in St Bernards, slipped discs in dachshunds, slipped kneecaps in toy poodles and dislocated hips in Alsatians.

Sharks can smell one part blood in 100 million parts of water.

An average 70-year-old American has eaten 14 cattle, 12 sheep, 23 pigs, 2 calves, 880 chickens, 35 turkeys, and 770lb. of fish.

Penicillin kills guinea pigs.

King George V's constant companion was a grey-pink parrot called Charlotte.

Archer fish catch insects by shooting them down with drops of water.

It takes more than 20,000 fishes to feed four great crested grebe chicks for twelve weeks.

Mr James Piper of Virginia Water, Surrey, had to call the fire brigade to get his horse Whizzer out of a neighbour's apple tree after a motor-cycle backfired.

A robust lover, the male scorpion deposits his sperm on the ground and drags his mate over it with his pincers.

The mugger is an Indian crocodile. Fifty are kept in sacred memory of a Muslim saint near Karachi.

Zoo flamingoes must have regular helpings of a certain type of shrimp or their glamorous pink plumage begins to fade.

Hopping and lolloping are the only forms of locomotion known to rabbits and hares. They cannot walk.

Skunks make no attempt to avoid oncoming cars. They stand their ground and rely on their foul-smelling spray.

The bull seal who sires the most offspring is the one who can go longest without food – dominant males never eat in the breeding season and may have to beat off rivals for as much as two months.

There are seven laying-out rooms at the Farmingdale Animals' Funeral Home in Long Island, N.Y., including the ultra-feminine Powder Puff Room for poodles and kittens; the Ming Room for Siamese cats and pekes; the Colonial Room, with rocking chairs, for collies; and – for all cats – the Purr-sian Room.

An Oxfordshire shepherd intends to boost Britain's exports by producing bi-lingual sheep-dogs. He is teaching his animals French.

Andy Robbins, 35-year-old British mid-heavyweight wrestling champion, had the claws removed from Hercules, a 10-month-old brown bear cub, in order to wrestle him in the ring. 'It's my best gimmick yet,' said Robbins after Hercules was granted a Performing Animal's Licence by Stirling District Council.

White-haired cats have an inbred tendency to deafness.

A five-dollar prize, offered by a travelling showman in the United States to anyone who could hold a chimp's shoulder to the ground for five seconds, was never won. Even professional wrestlers failed to meet the challenge.

A woman in the USA reared a pet eagle which laid eggs and invited her to sit on them.

The British sea cucumber foils attackers by entangling them in sticky threads shot from its anus.

Partridges allow themselves to be buried by falling snow to keep warm in severe winters.

A New York university professor has his dog's name entered in the telephone directory.

Only female mosquitoes bite humans.

A court at Selvio, northern Italy, convicted the local fieldmice of damaging valuable food crops in 1519. Despite the efforts of a lawyer engaged to defend the animals, they were sentenced to immediate banishment. Mercy was shown, however; the fieldmice were to be given safe conduct on their journey into exile. The town dogs and cats had to be restrained and bridges were built over streams to ease the way. Elderly mice and nursing mothers were granted an extra 14 days to prepare for the journey.

The nectar of one type of rhododendron is so potent that it makes bees drop to the ground and fall asleep.

Cobra mating lasts anything from two minutes to 24 hours.

Japanese cabaret artist Miss Ongawa entertained audiences by inserting a live snake into her mouth and guiding it so that the head poked out of her nostril. As a finale, she ate the snake alive.

Jennifer Robertson of Argyllshire could clear a two-foot hurdle on her jumping cow Manda.

At Aix-en-Provence in the 19th century, townspeople celebrated the festival of Corpus Christi by kneeling and offering flowers to the 'finest tomcat in the country'. The lucky animal was dressed in baby clothes for the day.

Spider crabs camouflage themselves by transplanting robes of seaweed on to their backs.

Classical authors believed that worm lizards had a head at each end and that one head woke the other when it was time to change egg-guarding shifts.

Prawns can walk forwards but can swim only backwards.

The pupils of parrots' eyes contract when they talk.

Angus cattle generally dominate Shorthorns who, in their turn, can lord it over Herefords.

African goliath beetles grow as big as a man's fist.

Aristotle believed swallows hibernated in heaps at the bottoms of rivers.

Larvae of the freshwater eel grow from $\frac{1}{4}$in. to 3in. during the three years it takes them to cross the Atlantic from their spawning grounds in the Sargasso sea.

The phoney gorilla used in the film *Mighty Joe Young* had two hind feet where its hands should have been.